Gratitude Journal
16 weeks

www.gratitudeandmore.ca

Having enjoyed journaling for many years, I wanted something more than blank space to write out my gratitude list. This journal was created to help you *want* to journal every day.

Journaling can be very transformative. With this in mind, you are prompted with daily questions—questions that have an impact on your physical, emotional and spiritual well-being.

Each day is two pages, one with daily prompts and one lined page for any additional writing. There is also a Weekly Check-In page that allows you to review the previous week and set your intention for the coming days.

I hope you enjoy your journey over the next sixteen weeks. A grateful life is a happy life.

For more information on the wide variety of journals we offer, visit us at www.gratitudeandmore.ca

Journal—see where it takes you!

Leah

WEEKLY CHECK-IN

My Intention for Next Week:

I would like to:

go through old clothes / purge them.

Experience...

peace of mind

Let go of...

constantly picking myself apart

Feel...

Energetic

Learn to...

do something new at yoga

Stop...

doubting my self.

I want more of...	I want less of...
Connection	doubt
happiness.	fear
stability.	anger

Date:	Mood/Happiness Scale (1-10):
Jan 01/2023	AM 6　　　　PM 7
Did I spend time with those I love? At work - clients - coworkers Facetime - Aubretia	Was I fully present? Mostly.

I am grateful for:

Another new years day clean.

To feel safe and healthy

That I have a warm home to be in ♡

That I don't need anything.

How did I enrich my spiritual life? Connecting with others at work	How did I move my body today? just by working.

Did I nourish my body and drink enough water?

I ate fruits and veggies - could have
drank more water and WAY less coffee.

What do I need to work on? - Spiritual - physical	Did I express myself creatively? Not really..

Did I spend responsibly? $0	Today's highlights: Slept well last night ☺ new years day.
Was I generous and kind? (to me too) I could have been kinder.	

my goal is to joural and to
see if it helps sort out
my emotions, which I
know it will. I don't take
enough time in every day
to do things like this.
I'm looking forward to
having an outlet, I'm
unsure why I've been
so hesitant to consistently
write. I often feel like
I don't have much to say
I guess but I'm left
with alot in my mind.
I have a lot of goals for
myself and my future
sometimes so much so that
I overwhelm myself thinking
about it but I'm greatful
for that because there was
a time I didn't want a future

I am comfortable in my body and all is well.

Date:	Mood/Happiness Scale (1-10):
Jan 04/23	AM 6 PM 6
Did I spend time with those I love?	**Was I fully present?**
Called bresha try melissa.	ISh.

I am grateful for:

having enough money for my new bed
to be able to get groceries whenever
that I feel sane and at peace
my body

How did I enrich my spiritual life?	**How did I move my body today?**
I connect to mom every day when I think of her?	evercised for 45 mins.

Did I nourish my body and drink enough water?

- Ate good food
- could have drank more water.

What do I need to work on?	**Did I express myself creatively?**
• more water • balanced eating • Spiritual	I put my new bed together.

Did I spend responsibly?	**Today's highlights:**
just bought groceries $50.	• New bed. • Started organizing bedroom.
Was I generous and kind? (to me too)	
Yes. to others I was helpful	°

I feel overwhelmed with the amount of organizing I have to do and the things I have to sort through and get rid of. My mind is so much more peaceful with less clutter. Obviously. It's just a battle to allow myself to get rid of things and I don't have a lot of space to either store things or get rid of them. I just want to purge as much as I can so that thing can feel simple, so I can keep things clean. I don't wear most clothes or use most of the things that I have.

Ruach: An explosive, expansive, surprising, creative energy that surges through all things. (Ancient Hebrew)

Date:	Mood/Happiness Scale (1-10):
Jan 9/23.	AM 5 PM 5
Did I spend time with those I love?	**Was I fully present?**
Over facetime / at work.	ish .

I am grateful for:

Clean clothes.

a comfy bed

memories

that I'm breathing.

How did I enrich my spiritual life?	How did I move my body today?
yoga ♡	yoga ? .

Did I nourish my body and drink enough water?

Over ate - at work chocolate and snack, not enough water.

What do I need to work on?	Did I express myself creatively?
• eating. • going outside more	NO .
Did I spend responsibly? $ 0	**Today's highlights:** • work. • napped. •
Was I generous and kind? (to me too) could have been nicer.	

Writing from yesterday did my usual yoga in the morning with Melissa, napped and went to work. Work was alot which seems to be the theme lately. I've been quite negative about it and I'm trying to change my part in it, but I'm feeling frusterated about certain aspects of the job that are inconsistent. I'm trying to not feel resentful and to feel graditude toward my job because its given me alot but I can't seem to shake certain things that aren't right about it.

To thine own self be true. (William Shakespeare)

Date: Jan 11 /23.	Mood/Happiness Scale (1-10): AM 6 PM 7
Did I spend time with those I love? yes.	Was I fully present? Kinda.

I am grateful for:

a healthy body.

being able to be vulnerable.

having a safe, cozy home.

that I'm clean and sober.

How did I enrich my spiritual life? Went to a meeting	How did I move my body today? TRX.

Did I nourish my body and drink enough water?

Overate, not enough water

Still struggling in that area

What do I need to work on?	Did I express myself creatively?
• food. • budget. • long term goals	NO.

Did I spend responsibly? approx $90	Today's highlights: • excercised • meeting. • coffee w Christina
Was I generous and kind? (to me too) yes.	

I'm putting more focus on going to meetings, went to one tonight which was really good. I've found that I am much more comfortable shareing. I need to take a hard look at my finances. decide about trading in my car. rework some of my bills and do some budgeting to see if it will be do able to get invisilyn. That and looking into school is my main goal right now. I'm not making a humble wage but I want to own my own home one day and I wont be able to with the money I'm making.

Date:	Mood/Happiness Scale (1-10): AM PM
Did I spend time with those I love?	Was I fully present?
I am grateful for:	
How did I enrich my spiritual life?	How did I move my body today?
Did I nourish my body and drink enough water?	
What do I need to work on?	Did I express myself creatively?
Did I spend responsibly?	Today's highlights:
Was I generous and kind? (to me too)	

Abundance flows through me. I am a channel for the Universe.

Date:	Mood/Happiness Scale (1-10): AM PM
Did I spend time with those I love?	Was I fully present?
I am grateful for:	
How did I enrich my spiritual life?	How did I move my body today?
Did I nourish my body and drink enough water?	
What do I need to work on?	Did I express myself creatively?
Did I spend responsibly?	Today's highlights:
Was I generous and kind? (to me too)	

Rise! Do not shrink.

| Date: | Mood/Happiness Scale (1-10): |
	AM PM
Did I spend time with those I love?	Was I fully present?
I am grateful for:	
How did I enrich my spiritual life?	How did I move my body today?
Did I nourish my body and drink enough water?	
What do I need to work on?	Did I express myself creatively?
Did I spend responsibly?	Today's highlights:
Was I generous and kind? (to me too)	

You are worthy. You are important. You are loved.

REVIEW OF LAST WEEK

How balanced was my time? (work/family/Me)	Did I get outside every day for fresh air?
Did I have the support I needed?	Did I ask for help when I needed it?

Did I remember my intentions from last week?

Did I spend enough time being unplugged?

I am proud that I....

Notes:

WEEKLY CHECK-IN

My Intention for Next Week:

I would like to:

Experience...

Let go of...

Feel...

Learn to...

Stop...

I want more of...	I want less of...

Date:	Mood/Happiness Scale (1-10): AM PM
Did I spend time with those I love?	Was I fully present?
I am grateful for:	
How did I enrich my spiritual life?	How did I move my body today?
Did I nourish my body and drink enough water?	
What do I need to work on?	Did I express myself creatively?
Did I spend responsibly?	Today's highlights:
Was I generous and kind? (to me too)	

The Universe is conspiring with you, never against you.

Date:	Mood/Happiness Scale (1-10): AM PM
Did I spend time with those I love?	Was I fully present?
I am grateful for:	
How did I enrich my spiritual life?	How did I move my body today?
Did I nourish my body and drink enough water?	
What do I need to work on?	Did I express myself creatively?
Did I spend responsibly?	Today's highlights:
Was I generous and kind? (to me too)	

All that I seek is already within me.

Date:	Mood/Happiness Scale (1-10): AM PM
Did I spend time with those I love?	Was I fully present?
I am grateful for:	
How did I enrich my spiritual life?	How did I move my body today?
Did I nourish my body and drink enough water?	
What do I need to work on?	Did I express myself creatively?
Did I spend responsibly?	Today's highlights:
Was I generous and kind? (to me too)	

I am guided by my intention. I am open to the Universe.

Date:	Mood/Happiness Scale (1-10): AM PM
Did I spend time with those I love?	Was I fully present?
I am grateful for:	
How did I enrich my spiritual life?	How did I move my body today?
Did I nourish my body and drink enough water?	
What do I need to work on?	Did I express myself creatively?
Did I spend responsibly?	Today's highlights:
Was I generous and kind? (to me too)	

I am unlimited. My life is filled with abundance.

Date:	Mood/Happiness Scale (1-10):
	AM PM
Did I spend time with those I love?	Was I fully present?
I am grateful for:	
How did I enrich my spiritual life?	How did I move my body today?
Did I nourish my body and drink enough water?	
What do I need to work on?	Did I express myself creatively?
Did I spend responsibly?	Today's highlights:
Was I generous and kind? (to me too)	

I have freed myself from fear and self-doubt.

Date:	Mood/Happiness Scale (1-10): AM PM
Did I spend time with those I love?	Was I fully present?
I am grateful for:	
How did I enrich my spiritual life?	How did I move my body today?
Did I nourish my body and drink enough water?	
What do I need to work on?	Did I express myself creatively?
Did I spend responsibly?	Today's highlights:
Was I generous and kind? (to me too)	

I am in sync. I flow with the river of life.

Date:	Mood/Happiness Scale (1-10): AM PM
Did I spend time with those I love?	Was I fully present?
I am grateful for:	
How did I enrich my spiritual life?	How did I move my body today?
Did I nourish my body and drink enough water?	
What do I need to work on?	Did I express myself creatively?
Did I spend responsibly?	Today's highlights:
Was I generous and kind? (to me too)	

I choose to release fear, anger, hurt and resentment.

REVIEW OF LAST WEEK

How balanced was my time? (work/family/Me)	Did I get outside every day for fresh air?
Did I have the support I needed?	Did I ask for help when I needed it?

Did I remember my intentions from last week?

Did I spend enough time being unplugged?

I am proud that I....

Notes:

WEEKLY CHECK-IN

My Intention for Next Week:

I would like to:

Experience...

Let go of...

Feel...

Learn to...

Stop...

I want more of...	I want less of...

Date:	Mood/Happiness Scale (1-10):
	AM PM
Did I spend time with those I love?	Was I fully present?
I am grateful for:	
How did I enrich my spiritual life?	How did I move my body today?
Did I nourish my body and drink enough water?	
What do I need to work on?	Did I express myself creatively?
Did I spend responsibly?	Today's highlights:
Was I generous and kind? (to me too)	

I forgive others; I love myself and deserve the freedom it brings.

Date:	Mood/Happiness Scale (1-10): AM PM
Did I spend time with those I love?	Was I fully present?

I am grateful for:

How did I enrich my spiritual life?	How did I move my body today?

Did I nourish my body and drink enough water?

What do I need to work on?	Did I express myself creatively?
Did I spend responsibly?	Today's highlights:
Was I generous and kind? (to me too)	

How do you act authentically?

Date:	Mood/Happiness Scale (1-10):
	AM PM
Did I spend time with those I love?	Was I fully present?
I am grateful for:	
How did I enrich my spiritual life?	How did I move my body today?
Did I nourish my body and drink enough water?	
What do I need to work on?	Did I express myself creatively?
Did I spend responsibly?	Today's highlights:
Was I generous and kind? (to me too)	

I am open to new experiences and new people.

Date:	Mood/Happiness Scale (1-10):
	AM PM
Did I spend time with those I love?	Was I fully present?

I am grateful for:

How did I enrich my spiritual life?	How did I move my body today?

Did I nourish my body and drink enough water?

What do I need to work on?	Did I express myself creatively?

Did I spend responsibly?	Today's highlights:
Was I generous and kind? (to me too)	

Be still and know that I am God. (Psalm 46:10)

Date:	Mood/Happiness Scale (1-10): AM PM
Did I spend time with those I love?	Was I fully present?
I am grateful for:	
How did I enrich my spiritual life?	How did I move my body today?
Did I nourish my body and drink enough water?	
What do I need to work on?	Did I express myself creatively?
Did I spend responsibly?	Today's highlights:
Was I generous and kind? (to me too)	

I am patient, tolerant and filled with compassion.

| Date: | Mood/Happiness Scale (1-10): |
	AM PM
Did I spend time with those I love?	Was I fully present?

I am grateful for:

How did I enrich my spiritual life?	How did I move my body today?

Did I nourish my body and drink enough water?

What do I need to work on?	Did I express myself creatively?

Did I spend responsibly?	Today's highlights:
Was I generous and kind? (to me too)	

I love every cell of my beautiful self.

Date:	Mood/Happiness Scale (1-10): AM PM
Did I spend time with those I love?	Was I fully present?
I am grateful for:	
How did I enrich my spiritual life?	How did I move my body today?
Did I nourish my body and drink enough water?	
What do I need to work on?	Did I express myself creatively?
Did I spend responsibly?	Today's highlights:
Was I generous and kind? (to me too)	

I am protected and safe.

REVIEW OF LAST WEEK

How balanced was my time? (work/family/Me)	Did I get outside every day for fresh air?
Did I have the support I needed?	Did I ask for help when I needed it?

Did I remember my intentions from last week?

Did I spend enough time being unplugged?

I am proud that I....

Notes:

WEEKLY CHECK-IN

My Intention for Next Week:

I would like to:

Experience...

Let go of...

Feel...

Learn to...

Stop...

I want more of...	I want less of...

| Date: | Mood/Happiness Scale (1-10): |
	AM PM
Did I spend time with those I love?	Was I fully present?
I am grateful for:	
How did I enrich my spiritual life?	How did I move my body today?
Did I nourish my body and drink enough water?	
What do I need to work on?	Did I express myself creatively?
Did I spend responsibly?	Today's highlights:
Was I generous and kind? (to me too)	

My body is strong and supports me in all I do.

Date:	Mood/Happiness Scale (1-10): AM PM
Did I spend time with those I love?	Was I fully present?

I am grateful for:

How did I enrich my spiritual life?	How did I move my body today?

Did I nourish my body and drink enough water?

What do I need to work on?	Did I express myself creatively?

Did I spend responsibly?	Today's highlights:
Was I generous and kind? (to me too)	

My life is unfolding with ease.

Date:	Mood/Happiness Scale (1-10):
	AM PM

Did I spend time with those I love?	Was I fully present?

I am grateful for:	

How did I enrich my spiritual life?	How did I move my body today?

Did I nourish my body and drink enough water?	

What do I need to work on?	Did I express myself creatively?

Did I spend responsibly?	Today's highlights:
Was I generous and kind? (to me too)	

My days are filled with excitement and love.

Date:	Mood/Happiness Scale (1-10): AM PM
Did I spend time with those I love?	Was I fully present?
I am grateful for:	
How did I enrich my spiritual life?	How did I move my body today?
Did I nourish my body and drink enough water?	
What do I need to work on?	Did I express myself creatively?
Did I spend responsibly?	Today's highlights:
Was I generous and kind? (to me too)	

Serenity is not the absence of conflict, but the ability to cope with it.

| Date: | Mood/Happiness Scale (1-10): |
	AM PM
Did I spend time with those I love?	Was I fully present?
I am grateful for:	
How did I enrich my spiritual life?	How did I move my body today?
Did I nourish my body and drink enough water?	
What do I need to work on?	Did I express myself creatively?
Did I spend responsibly?	Today's highlights:
Was I generous and kind? (to me too)	

At the center of your being you have the answer; you know who you are and you know what you want. (Lao Tzu)

Date:	Mood/Happiness Scale (1-10): AM PM
Did I spend time with those I love?	Was I fully present?
I am grateful for:	
How did I enrich my spiritual life?	How did I move my body today?
Did I nourish my body and drink enough water?	
What do I need to work on?	Did I express myself creatively?
Did I spend responsibly?	Today's highlights:
Was I generous and kind? (to me too)	

Everyone has a story. It's not how you tell it. It's how you live it.

Date:	Mood/Happiness Scale (1-10):
	AM PM
Did I spend time with those I love?	Was I fully present?
I am grateful for:	
How did I enrich my spiritual life?	How did I move my body today?
Did I nourish my body and drink enough water?	
What do I need to work on?	Did I express myself creatively?
Did I spend responsibly?	Today's highlights:
Was I generous and kind? (to me too)	

The two most important days in your life are the day you were born and the day you find out why. (Mark Twain)

REVIEW OF LAST WEEK

How balanced was my time? (work/family/Me)	Did I get outside every day for fresh air?
Did I have the support I needed?	Did I ask for help when I needed it?

Did I remember my intentions from last week?

Did I spend enough time being unplugged?

I am proud that I....

Notes:

WEEKLY CHECK-IN

My Intention for Next Week:

I would like to:

Experience...

Let go of...

Feel...

Learn to...

Stop...

I want more of...	I want less of...

Date:	Mood/Happiness Scale (1-10):
	AM PM
Did I spend time with those I love?	Was I fully present?
I am grateful for:	
How did I enrich my spiritual life?	How did I move my body today?
Did I nourish my body and drink enough water?	
What do I need to work on?	Did I express myself creatively?
Did I spend responsibly?	Today's highlights:
Was I generous and kind? (to me too)	

The task ahead of us is never as great as the Power behind us.
(Ralph Waldo Emerson)

| Date: | Mood/Happiness Scale (1-10): |
| | AM   PM |

| Did I spend time with those I love? | Was I fully present? |

I am grateful for:

| How did I enrich my spiritual life? | How did I move my body today? |

Did I nourish my body and drink enough water?

| What do I need to work on? | Did I express myself creatively? |

| Did I spend responsibly? | Today's highlights: |

Was I generous and kind? (to me too)

It's all an inside job.

| Date: | Mood/Happiness Scale (1-10): |
	AM PM
Did I spend time with those I love?	Was I fully present?

I am grateful for:

How did I enrich my spiritual life?	How did I move my body today?

Did I nourish my body and drink enough water?

What do I need to work on?	Did I express myself creatively?

Did I spend responsibly?	Today's highlights:
Was I generous and kind? (to me too)	

Do you want to be right or do you want to be happy?

Date:	Mood/Happiness Scale (1-10): AM PM
Did I spend time with those I love?	Was I fully present?
I am grateful for:	
How did I enrich my spiritual life?	How did I move my body today?
Did I nourish my body and drink enough water?	
What do I need to work on?	Did I express myself creatively?
Did I spend responsibly?	Today's highlights:
Was I generous and kind? (to me too)	

Each new day offers twenty-four hours of possibility and
moves you forward on your path.

| Date: | Mood/Happiness Scale (1-10): |
	AM PM
Did I spend time with those I love?	Was I fully present?
I am grateful for:	
How did I enrich my spiritual life?	How did I move my body today?
Did I nourish my body and drink enough water?	
What do I need to work on?	Did I express myself creatively?
Did I spend responsibly?	Today's highlights:
Was I generous and kind? (to me too)	

Each day may not be good, but there is good in every day. (Alice Earle)

Date:	Mood/Happiness Scale (1-10): AM PM
Did I spend time with those I love?	Was I fully present?
I am grateful for:	
How did I enrich my spiritual life?	How did I move my body today?
Did I nourish my body and drink enough water?	
What do I need to work on?	Did I express myself creatively?
Did I spend responsibly?	Today's highlights:
Was I generous and kind? (to me too)	

The first step towards getting somewhere is to decide that you are not going to stay where you are.

Date:	Mood/Happiness Scale (1-10): AM PM
Did I spend time with those I love?	Was I fully present?
I am grateful for:	
How did I enrich my spiritual life?	How did I move my body today?
Did I nourish my body and drink enough water?	
What do I need to work on?	Did I express myself creatively?
Did I spend responsibly?	Today's highlights:
Was I generous and kind? (to me too)	

_It's not about being the best, it's about being better
than you were yesterday._

REVIEW OF LAST WEEK

How balanced was my time? (work/family/Me)	Did I get outside every day for fresh air?
Did I have the support I needed?	Did I ask for help when I needed it?

Did I remember my intentions from last week?

Did I spend enough time being unplugged?

I am proud that I....

Notes:

WEEKLY CHECK-IN

My Intention for Next Week:

I would like to:

Experience...

Let go of...

Feel...

Learn to...

Stop...

I want more of...	I want less of...

| Date: | Mood/Happiness Scale (1-10): |
| | AM   PM |

| Did I spend time with those I love? | Was I fully present? |

I am grateful for:

| How did I enrich my spiritual life? | How did I move my body today? |

Did I nourish my body and drink enough water?

| What do I need to work on? | Did I express myself creatively? |

| Did I spend responsibly? | Today's highlights: |

| Was I generous and kind? (to me too) | |

The mind is slow in unlearning what it has been long in learning. (Seneca)

Date:	Mood/Happiness Scale (1-10): AM PM
Did I spend time with those I love?	Was I fully present?
I am grateful for:	
How did I enrich my spiritual life?	How did I move my body today?
Did I nourish my body and drink enough water?	
What do I need to work on?	Did I express myself creatively?
Did I spend responsibly?	Today's highlights:
Was I generous and kind? (to me too)	

Be ready at any moment to sacrifice what you are
for what you could become. (Charles Dubois)

| Date: | Mood/Happiness Scale (1-10): |
	AM PM
Did I spend time with those I love?	Was I fully present?
I am grateful for:	
How did I enrich my spiritual life?	How did I move my body today?
Did I nourish my body and drink enough water?	
What do I need to work on?	Did I express myself creatively?
Did I spend responsibly?	Today's highlights:
Was I generous and kind? (to me too)	

When one is willing and eager, the gods join in. (Aeschylus)

Date:	Mood/Happiness Scale (1-10): AM PM
Did I spend time with those I love?	Was I fully present?
I am grateful for:	
How did I enrich my spiritual life?	How did I move my body today?
Did I nourish my body and drink enough water?	
What do I need to work on?	Did I express myself creatively?
Did I spend responsibly?	Today's highlights:
Was I generous and kind? (to me too)	

The real voyage of discovery consists not in seeing new landscapes,
but in having new eyes. (Marcel Proust)

Date:	Mood/Happiness Scale (1-10): AM PM
Did I spend time with those I love?	Was I fully present?
I am grateful for:	
How did I enrich my spiritual life?	How did I move my body today?
Did I nourish my body and drink enough water?	
What do I need to work on?	Did I express myself creatively?
Did I spend responsibly?	Today's highlights:
Was I generous and kind? (to me too)	

There is no way to happiness. Happiness is the way. (Thich Nhat Hanh)

Date:	Mood/Happiness Scale (1-10):
	AM PM
Did I spend time with those I love?	Was I fully present?
I am grateful for:	
How did I enrich my spiritual life?	How did I move my body today?
Did I nourish my body and drink enough water?	
What do I need to work on?	Did I express myself creatively?
Did I spend responsibly?	Today's highlights:
Was I generous and kind? (to me too)	

Be the change you want to see in the world. (Mahatma Gandhi)

Date:	Mood/Happiness Scale (1-10): AM PM
Did I spend time with those I love?	Was I fully present?
I am grateful for:	
How did I enrich my spiritual life?	How did I move my body today?
Did I nourish my body and drink enough water?	
What do I need to work on?	Did I express myself creatively?
Did I spend responsibly?	Today's highlights:
Was I generous and kind? (to me too)	

If the only prayer you ever say in your whole life is "thank you",
that would suffice. (Meister Eckhart)

REVIEW OF LAST WEEK

How balanced was my time? (work/family/Me)	Did I get outside every day for fresh air?
Did I have the support I needed?	Did I ask for help when I needed it?

Did I remember my intentions from last week?

Did I spend enough time being unplugged?

I am proud that I....

Notes:

WEEKLY CHECK-IN

My Intention for Next Week:

I would like to:

Experience...

Let go of...

Feel...

Learn to...

Stop...

I want more of...	I want less of...

| Date: | Mood/Happiness Scale (1-10): |
| | AM   PM |

| Did I spend time with those I love? | Was I fully present? |

I am grateful for:

| How did I enrich my spiritual life? | How did I move my body today? |

Did I nourish my body and drink enough water?

| What do I need to work on? | Did I express myself creatively? |

| Did I spend responsibly? | Today's highlights: |

Was I generous and kind? (to me too)

Believe in miracles, but do the footwork.

Date:	Mood/Happiness Scale (1-10):
	AM PM
Did I spend time with those I love?	Was I fully present?
I am grateful for:	
How did I enrich my spiritual life?	How did I move my body today?
Did I nourish my body and drink enough water?	
What do I need to work on?	Did I express myself creatively?
Did I spend responsibly?	Today's highlights:
Was I generous and kind? (to me too)	

Leave room—life's most treasured moments often come unannounced.

Date:	Mood/Happiness Scale (1-10): AM PM
Did I spend time with those I love?	Was I fully present?
I am grateful for:	
How did I enrich my spiritual life?	How did I move my body today?
Did I nourish my body and drink enough water?	
What do I need to work on?	Did I express myself creatively?
Did I spend responsibly?	Today's highlights:
Was I generous and kind? (to me too)	

Be willing to accept a temporary inconvenience for a permanent
improvement.

Date:	Mood/Happiness Scale (1-10): AM PM
Did I spend time with those I love?	Was I fully present?
I am grateful for:	
How did I enrich my spiritual life?	How did I move my body today?
Did I nourish my body and drink enough water?	
What do I need to work on?	Did I express myself creatively?
Did I spend responsibly?	Today's highlights:
Was I generous and kind? (to me too)	

Seek respect rather than popularity.

Date:	Mood/Happiness Scale (1-10):
	AM PM

Did I spend time with those I love?	Was I fully present?

I am grateful for:	

How did I enrich my spiritual life?	How did I move my body today?

Did I nourish my body and drink enough water?	

What do I need to work on?	Did I express myself creatively?

Did I spend responsibly?	Today's highlights:
Was I generous and kind? (to me too)	

Is what you're doing today getting you closer to where you want to be tomorrow?

Date:	Mood/Happiness Scale (1-10):
	AM PM
Did I spend time with those I love?	Was I fully present?

| I am grateful for: |

| How did I enrich my spiritual life? | How did I move my body today? |

| Did I nourish my body and drink enough water? |

| What do I need to work on? | Did I express myself creatively? |

| Did I spend responsibly? | Today's highlights: |
| Was I generous and kind? (to me too) | |

Belief is simply acceptance without proof.

| Date: | Mood/Happiness Scale (1-10): |
	AM PM
Did I spend time with those I love?	Was I fully present?
I am grateful for:	
How did I enrich my spiritual life?	How did I move my body today?
Did I nourish my body and drink enough water?	
What do I need to work on?	Did I express myself creatively?
Did I spend responsibly?	Today's highlights:
Was I generous and kind? (to me too)	

The only people with whom you should try to get even with are those who have helped you. (John E. Southard)

REVIEW OF LAST WEEK

How balanced was my time? (work/family/Me)	Did I get outside every day for fresh air?
Did I have the support I needed?	Did I ask for help when I needed it?

Did I remember my intentions from last week?

Did I spend enough time being unplugged?

I am proud that I....

Notes:

WEEKLY CHECK-IN

My Intention for Next Week:

I would like to:

Experience...

Let go of...

Feel...

Learn to...

Stop...

I want more of...	I want less of...

| Date: | Mood/Happiness Scale (1-10): |
	AM PM
Did I spend time with those I love?	Was I fully present?
I am grateful for:	
How did I enrich my spiritual life?	How did I move my body today?
Did I nourish my body and drink enough water?	
What do I need to work on?	Did I express myself creatively?
Did I spend responsibly?	Today's highlights:
Was I generous and kind? (to me too)	

Failure isn't being knocked down—it's staying down.

Date:	Mood/Happiness Scale (1-10):
	AM PM
Did I spend time with those I love?	Was I fully present?
I am grateful for:	
How did I enrich my spiritual life?	How did I move my body today?
Did I nourish my body and drink enough water?	
What do I need to work on?	Did I express myself creatively?
Did I spend responsibly?	Today's highlights:
Was I generous and kind? (to me too)	

What do you dream of when no one is watching?

Date:	Mood/Happiness Scale (1-10): AM PM
Did I spend time with those I love?	Was I fully present?

I am grateful for:

How did I enrich my spiritual life?	How did I move my body today?

Did I nourish my body and drink enough water?

What do I need to work on?	Did I express myself creatively?
Did I spend responsibly?	Today's highlights:
Was I generous and kind? (to me too)	

The more we resist, the more stuck we become.

Date:	Mood/Happiness Scale (1-10):
	AM PM
Did I spend time with those I love?	Was I fully present?
I am grateful for:	
How did I enrich my spiritual life?	How did I move my body today?
Did I nourish my body and drink enough water?	
What do I need to work on?	Did I express myself creatively?
Did I spend responsibly?	Today's highlights:
Was I generous and kind? (to me too)	

Start each day with a sense of possibility.

| Date: | Mood/Happiness Scale (1-10): |
	AM PM
Did I spend time with those I love?	Was I fully present?
I am grateful for:	
How did I enrich my spiritual life?	How did I move my body today?
Did I nourish my body and drink enough water?	
What do I need to work on?	Did I express myself creatively?
Did I spend responsibly?	Today's highlights:
Was I generous and kind? (to me too)	

The same boiling water that softens the potato hardens the egg. It's about what you're made of, not the circumstances. (Unknown)

Date:	Mood/Happiness Scale (1-10): AM PM
Did I spend time with those I love?	Was I fully present?
I am grateful for:	
How did I enrich my spiritual life?	How did I move my body today?
Did I nourish my body and drink enough water?	
What do I need to work on?	Did I express myself creatively?
Did I spend responsibly?	Today's highlights:
Was I generous and kind? (to me too)	

We know what we are but know not what we may be. (William Shakespeare)

Date:	Mood/Happiness Scale (1-10): AM PM
Did I spend time with those I love?	Was I fully present?
I am grateful for:	
How did I enrich my spiritual life?	How did I move my body today?
Did I nourish my body and drink enough water?	
What do I need to work on?	Did I express myself creatively?
Did I spend responsibly?	Today's highlights:
Was I generous and kind? (to me too)	

I care not so much what I am to others as what I am to myself.
(Michel Eyquem de Montaigne)

REVIEW OF LAST WEEK

How balanced was my time? (work/family/Me)	Did I get outside every day for fresh air?
Did I have the support I needed?	Did I ask for help when I needed it?

Did I remember my intentions from last week?

Did I spend enough time being unplugged?

I am proud that I....

Notes:

WEEKLY CHECK-IN

My Intention for Next Week:

I would like to:

Experience...

Let go of...

Feel...

Learn to...

Stop...

I want more of...	I want less of...

Date:	Mood/Happiness Scale (1-10):
	AM PM
Did I spend time with those I love?	Was I fully present?

I am grateful for:

How did I enrich my spiritual life?	How did I move my body today?

Did I nourish my body and drink enough water?

What do I need to work on?	Did I express myself creatively?
Did I spend responsibly?	Today's highlights:
Was I generous and kind? (to me too)	

We are what we do, not what we say we do.

Date:	Mood/Happiness Scale (1-10): AM PM
Did I spend time with those I love?	Was I fully present?
I am grateful for:	
How did I enrich my spiritual life?	How did I move my body today?
Did I nourish my body and drink enough water?	
What do I need to work on?	Did I express myself creatively?
Did I spend responsibly?	Today's highlights:
Was I generous and kind? (to me too)	

Let your faith be bigger than your fear.

Date:	Mood/Happiness Scale (1-10):
	AM PM
Did I spend time with those I love?	Was I fully present?

I am grateful for:

How did I enrich my spiritual life?	How did I move my body today?

Did I nourish my body and drink enough water?

What do I need to work on?	Did I express myself creatively?
Did I spend responsibly?	Today's highlights:
Was I generous and kind? (to me too)	

Do the next right thing.

Date:	Mood/Happiness Scale (1-10): AM PM
Did I spend time with those I love?	Was I fully present?
I am grateful for:	
How did I enrich my spiritual life?	How did I move my body today?
Did I nourish my body and drink enough water?	
What do I need to work on?	Did I express myself creatively?
Did I spend responsibly?	Today's highlights:
Was I generous and kind? (to me too)	

Don't complain about the things you're not willing to change.

Date:	Mood/Happiness Scale (1-10): AM PM
Did I spend time with those I love?	Was I fully present?
I am grateful for:	
How did I enrich my spiritual life?	How did I move my body today?
Did I nourish my body and drink enough water?	
What do I need to work on?	Did I express myself creatively?
Did I spend responsibly?	Today's highlights:
Was I generous and kind? (to me too)	

You are not here to figure out your life, you are here to create it.

| Date: | Mood/Happiness Scale (1-10): |
	AM PM
Did I spend time with those I love?	Was I fully present?
I am grateful for:	
How did I enrich my spiritual life?	How did I move my body today?
Did I nourish my body and drink enough water?	
What do I need to work on?	Did I express myself creatively?
Did I spend responsibly?	Today's highlights:
Was I generous and kind? (to me too)	

Stop worrying about what can go wrong and
get excited about what can go right.

Date:	Mood/Happiness Scale (1-10): AM PM
Did I spend time with those I love?	Was I fully present?

I am grateful for:

How did I enrich my spiritual life?	How did I move my body today?

Did I nourish my body and drink enough water?

What do I need to work on?	Did I express myself creatively?

Did I spend responsibly?	Today's highlights:
Was I generous and kind? (to me too)	

If there is no change, there is no change.

REVIEW OF LAST WEEK

How balanced was my time? (work/family/Me)	Did I get outside every day for fresh air?
Did I have the support I needed?	Did I ask for help when I needed it?

Did I remember my intentions from last week?

Did I spend enough time being unplugged?

I am proud that I....

Notes:

WEEKLY CHECK-IN

My Intention for Next Week:

I would like to:

Experience...

Let go of...

Feel...

Learn to...

Stop...

I want more of...	I want less of...

Date:	Mood/Happiness Scale (1-10):
	AM PM
Did I spend time with those I love?	Was I fully present?
I am grateful for:	
How did I enrich my spiritual life?	How did I move my body today?
Did I nourish my body and drink enough water?	
What do I need to work on?	Did I express myself creatively?
Did I spend responsibly?	Today's highlights:
Was I generous and kind? (to me too)	

Life: It's the greatest journey you will ever be on.

Date:	Mood/Happiness Scale (1-10): AM PM
Did I spend time with those I love?	Was I fully present?
I am grateful for:	
How did I enrich my spiritual life?	How did I move my body today?
Did I nourish my body and drink enough water?	
What do I need to work on?	Did I express myself creatively?
Did I spend responsibly?	Today's highlights:
Was I generous and kind? (to me too)	

You are today where your thoughts have brought you; you will be tomorrow where your thoughts take you. (James Allen)

Date:	Mood/Happiness Scale (1-10): AM PM
Did I spend time with those I love?	Was I fully present?
I am grateful for:	
How did I enrich my spiritual life?	How did I move my body today?
Did I nourish my body and drink enough water?	
What do I need to work on?	Did I express myself creatively?
Did I spend responsibly?	Today's highlights:
Was I generous and kind? (to me too)	

Most people are about as happy as they make up their minds to be.
(Abraham Lincoln)

Date:	Mood/Happiness Scale (1-10): AM PM
Did I spend time with those I love?	Was I fully present?
I am grateful for:	
How did I enrich my spiritual life?	How did I move my body today?
Did I nourish my body and drink enough water?	
What do I need to work on?	Did I express myself creatively?
Did I spend responsibly?	Today's highlights:
Was I generous and kind? (to me too)	

The love of oneself is the beginning of a lifelong romance. (Oscar Wilde)

Date:	Mood/Happiness Scale (1-10):
	AM PM
Did I spend time with those I love?	Was I fully present?
I am grateful for:	
How did I enrich my spiritual life?	How did I move my body today?
Did I nourish my body and drink enough water?	
What do I need to work on?	Did I express myself creatively?
Did I spend responsibly?	Today's highlights:
Was I generous and kind? (to me too)	

To accomplish great things, we must not only act, but also dream, not only plan, but also believe. (Anatole France)

Date:	Mood/Happiness Scale (1-10):
	AM PM
Did I spend time with those I love?	Was I fully present?
I am grateful for:	
How did I enrich my spiritual life?	How did I move my body today?
Did I nourish my body and drink enough water?	
What do I need to work on?	Did I express myself creatively?
Did I spend responsibly?	Today's highlights:
Was I generous and kind? (to me too)	

Let yourself be silently drawn by the stronger pull of what you really love.
(Rumi)

Date:	Mood/Happiness Scale (1-10): AM PM
Did I spend time with those I love?	Was I fully present?
I am grateful for:	
How did I enrich my spiritual life?	How did I move my body today?
Did I nourish my body and drink enough water?	
What do I need to work on?	Did I express myself creatively?
Did I spend responsibly?	Today's highlights:
Was I generous and kind? (to me too)	

Start by doing what is necessary; then do what's possible; and suddenly you are doing the impossible. (St. Francis of Assisi)

REVIEW OF LAST WEEK

How balanced was my time? (work/family/Me)	Did I get outside every day for fresh air?
Did I have the support I needed?	Did I ask for help when I needed it?

Did I remember my intentions from last week?

Did I spend enough time being unplugged?

I am proud that I....

Notes:

WEEKLY CHECK-IN

My Intention for Next Week:

I would like to:

Experience...

Let go of...

Feel...

Learn to...

Stop...

I want more of...	I want less of...

Date:	Mood/Happiness Scale (1-10):
	AM PM

Did I spend time with those I love?	Was I fully present?

I am grateful for:	

How did I enrich my spiritual life?	How did I move my body today?

Did I nourish my body and drink enough water?	

What do I need to work on?	Did I express myself creatively?

Did I spend responsibly?	Today's highlights:
Was I generous and kind? (to me too)	

Maybe it's about unbecoming everything that isn't really you, so you can be
who you were meant to be in the first place. (Unknown)

Date:	Mood/Happiness Scale (1-10):
	AM PM
Did I spend time with those I love?	Was I fully present?
I am grateful for:	
How did I enrich my spiritual life?	How did I move my body today?
Did I nourish my body and drink enough water?	
What do I need to work on?	Did I express myself creatively?
Did I spend responsibly?	Today's highlights:
Was I generous and kind? (to me too)	

Life is really simple, but we insist on making it complicated. (Confucius)

Date:	Mood/Happiness Scale (1-10): AM PM
Did I spend time with those I love?	Was I fully present?
I am grateful for:	
How did I enrich my spiritual life?	How did I move my body today?
Did I nourish my body and drink enough water?	
What do I need to work on?	Did I express myself creatively?
Did I spend responsibly?	Today's highlights:
Was I generous and kind? (to me too)	

Very little is needed to make a happy life; it is all within yourself, in your way of thinking. (Marcus Aurelius)

Date:	Mood/Happiness Scale (1-10): AM PM
Did I spend time with those I love?	Was I fully present?
I am grateful for:	
How did I enrich my spiritual life?	How did I move my body today?
Did I nourish my body and drink enough water?	
What do I need to work on?	Did I express myself creatively?
Did I spend responsibly?	Today's highlights:
Was I generous and kind? (to me too)	

Let your dreams be bigger than your fears, your actions louder than your words and your faith stronger than your feelings. (Unknown)

| Date: | Mood/Happiness Scale (1-10): |
	AM PM
Did I spend time with those I love?	Was I fully present?
I am grateful for:	
How did I enrich my spiritual life?	How did I move my body today?
Did I nourish my body and drink enough water?	
What do I need to work on?	Did I express myself creatively?
Did I spend responsibly?	Today's highlights:
Was I generous and kind? (to me too)	

I am only one, but I am one. I cannot do everything, but I can do something and I will not let what I cannot do interfere with what I can do. (Edward Everett Hale)

Date:	Mood/Happiness Scale (1-10): AM PM
Did I spend time with those I love?	Was I fully present?
I am grateful for:	
How did I enrich my spiritual life?	How did I move my body today?
Did I nourish my body and drink enough water?	
What do I need to work on?	Did I express myself creatively?
Did I spend responsibly?	Today's highlights:
Was I generous and kind? (to me too)	

Tension is who you think you should be. Relaxation is who you are.
(Chinese Proverb)

Date:	Mood/Happiness Scale (1-10):
	AM PM
Did I spend time with those I love?	Was I fully present?
I am grateful for:	
How did I enrich my spiritual life?	How did I move my body today?
Did I nourish my body and drink enough water?	
What do I need to work on?	Did I express myself creatively?
Did I spend responsibly?	Today's highlights:
Was I generous and kind? (to me too)	

Go confidently in the direction of your dreams and live the life you have imagined. (Henry David Thoreau)

REVIEW OF LAST WEEK

How balanced was my time? (work/family/Me)	Did I get outside every day for fresh air?
Did I have the support I needed?	Did I ask for help when I needed it?

Did I remember my intentions from last week?

Did I spend enough time being unplugged?

I am proud that I....

Notes:

WEEKLY CHECK-IN

My Intention for Next Week:

I would like to:

Experience...

Let go of...

Feel...

Learn to...

Stop...

I want more of...	I want less of...

Date:	Mood/Happiness Scale (1-10): AM PM
Did I spend time with those I love?	Was I fully present?
I am grateful for:	
How did I enrich my spiritual life?	How did I move my body today?
Did I nourish my body and drink enough water?	
What do I need to work on?	Did I express myself creatively?
Did I spend responsibly?	Today's highlights:
Was I generous and kind? (to me too)	

You yourself, as much as anybody in the entire universe deserve your love and affection. (Buddha)

Date:	Mood/Happiness Scale (1-10):
	AM PM
Did I spend time with those I love?	Was I fully present?

I am grateful for:

| How did I enrich my spiritual life? | How did I move my body today? |

Did I nourish my body and drink enough water?

| What do I need to work on? | Did I express myself creatively? |

| Did I spend responsibly? | Today's highlights: |

| Was I generous and kind? (to me too) | |

Habit is a cable; we weave a thread of it each day, and at last we cannot break it. (Horace Mann)

| Date: | Mood/Happiness Scale (1-10): |
	AM PM
Did I spend time with those I love?	Was I fully present?
I am grateful for:	
How did I enrich my spiritual life?	How did I move my body today?
Did I nourish my body and drink enough water?	
What do I need to work on?	Did I express myself creatively?
Did I spend responsibly?	Today's highlights:
Was I generous and kind? (to me too)	

If a man wants his dreams to come true, he must wake them up. (Unknown)

Date:	Mood/Happiness Scale (1-10):
	AM PM
Did I spend time with those I love?	Was I fully present?

I am grateful for:

How did I enrich my spiritual life?	How did I move my body today?

Did I nourish my body and drink enough water?

What do I need to work on?	Did I express myself creatively?
Did I spend responsibly?	Today's highlights:
Was I generous and kind? (to me too)	

A comfort zone is a beautiful place, but nothing ever grows there.

| Date: | Mood/Happiness Scale (1-10): |
	AM PM
Did I spend time with those I love?	Was I fully present?

I am grateful for:

How did I enrich my spiritual life?	How did I move my body today?

Did I nourish my body and drink enough water?

What do I need to work on?	Did I express myself creatively?

Did I spend responsibly?	Today's highlights:
Was I generous and kind? (to me too)	

There is only one way to happiness and that is to cease worrying about things which are beyond the power of our will. (Epictetus)

Date:	Mood/Happiness Scale (1-10):
	AM PM
Did I spend time with those I love?	Was I fully present?
I am grateful for:	
How did I enrich my spiritual life?	How did I move my body today?
Did I nourish my body and drink enough water?	
What do I need to work on?	Did I express myself creatively?
Did I spend responsibly?	Today's highlights:
Was I generous and kind? (to me too)	

True happiness is...to enjoy the present, without anxious dependence upon the future. (Lucius Annaeus Seneca)

Date:	Mood/Happiness Scale (1-10):
	AM PM

Did I spend time with those I love?	Was I fully present?

I am grateful for:	

How did I enrich my spiritual life?	How did I move my body today?

Did I nourish my body and drink enough water?	

What do I need to work on?	Did I express myself creatively?

Did I spend responsibly?	Today's highlights:
Was I generous and kind? (to me too)	

Happiness is the consequence of personal effort...you have to participate relentlessly in the manifestations of your own blessings. (Elizabeth Gilbert)

REVIEW OF LAST WEEK

How balanced was my time? (work/family/Me)	Did I get outside every day for fresh air?
Did I have the support I needed?	Did I ask for help when I needed it?

Did I remember my intentions from last week?

Did I spend enough time being unplugged?

I am proud that I....

Notes:

WEEKLY CHECK-IN

My Intention for Next Week:

I would like to:

Experience...

Let go of...

Feel...

Learn to...

Stop...

I want more of...	I want less of...

Date:	Mood/Happiness Scale (1-10): AM PM
Did I spend time with those I love?	Was I fully present?
I am grateful for:	
How did I enrich my spiritual life?	How did I move my body today?
Did I nourish my body and drink enough water?	
What do I need to work on?	Did I express myself creatively?
Did I spend responsibly?	Today's highlights:
Was I generous and kind? (to me too)	

Rules for happiness: something to do, someone to love,
something to hope for. (Immanuel Kant)

Date:	Mood/Happiness Scale (1-10):
	AM PM
Did I spend time with those I love?	Was I fully present?
I am grateful for:	
How did I enrich my spiritual life?	How did I move my body today?
Did I nourish my body and drink enough water?	
What do I need to work on?	Did I express myself creatively?
Did I spend responsibly?	Today's highlights:
Was I generous and kind? (to me too)	

Just when the caterpillar thought the world was ending,
he turned into a butterfly. (Proverb)

| Date: | Mood/Happiness Scale (1-10): |
| | AM   PM |

| Did I spend time with those I love? | Was I fully present? |

I am grateful for:

| How did I enrich my spiritual life? | How did I move my body today? |

Did I nourish my body and drink enough water?

| What do I need to work on? | Did I express myself creatively? |

| Did I spend responsibly? | Today's highlights: |

Was I generous and kind? (to me too)

Don't be pushed by your problems, be led by your dreams.
(Ralph Waldo Emerson)

| Date: | Mood/Happiness Scale (1-10): |
	AM PM
Did I spend time with those I love?	Was I fully present?

I am grateful for:

How did I enrich my spiritual life?	How did I move my body today?

Did I nourish my body and drink enough water?

What do I need to work on?	Did I express myself creatively?

Did I spend responsibly?	Today's highlights:
Was I generous and kind? (to me too)	

What seems to us as bitter trials are often blessings in disguise.
(Oscar Wilde)

Date:	Mood/Happiness Scale (1-10):
	AM PM
Did I spend time with those I love?	Was I fully present?
I am grateful for:	
How did I enrich my spiritual life?	How did I move my body today?
Did I nourish my body and drink enough water?	
What do I need to work on?	Did I express myself creatively?
Did I spend responsibly?	Today's highlights:
Was I generous and kind? (to me too)	

The meaning of life is to find your gift. The purpose of life is to give it away.
(William Shakespeare)

| Date: | Mood/Happiness Scale (1-10): |
	AM PM
Did I spend time with those I love?	Was I fully present?
I am grateful for:	
How did I enrich my spiritual life?	How did I move my body today?
Did I nourish my body and drink enough water?	
What do I need to work on?	Did I express myself creatively?
Did I spend responsibly?	Today's highlights:
Was I generous and kind? (to me too)	

I find that the harder I work the more luck I seem to have. (Thomas Jefferson)

| Date: | Mood/Happiness Scale (1-10): |
| | AM   PM |

| Did I spend time with those I love? | Was I fully present? |

I am grateful for:

| How did I enrich my spiritual life? | How did I move my body today? |

Did I nourish my body and drink enough water?

| What do I need to work on? | Did I express myself creatively? |

| Did I spend responsibly? | Today's highlights: |

| Was I generous and kind? (to me too) | |

Courage is resistance to fear, mastery of fear—not absence of it.
(Mark Twain)

REVIEW OF LAST WEEK

How balanced was my time? (work/family/Me)	Did I get outside every day for fresh air?
Did I have the support I needed?	Did I ask for help when I needed it?

Did I remember my intentions from last week?

Did I spend enough time being unplugged?

I am proud that I....

Notes:

WEEKLY CHECK-IN

My Intention for Next Week:

I would like to:

Experience...

Let go of...

Feel...

Learn to...

Stop...

I want more of...	I want less of...

Date:	Mood/Happiness Scale (1-10):
	AM PM
Did I spend time with those I love?	Was I fully present?
I am grateful for:	
How did I enrich my spiritual life?	How did I move my body today?
Did I nourish my body and drink enough water?	
What do I need to work on?	Did I express myself creatively?
Did I spend responsibly?	Today's highlights:
Was I generous and kind? (to me too)	

Above all else, guard your heart, for everything you do flows from it.
(Proverbs 4:23)

Date:	Mood/Happiness Scale (1-10): AM PM
Did I spend time with those I love?	Was I fully present?
I am grateful for:	
How did I enrich my spiritual life?	How did I move my body today?
Did I nourish my body and drink enough water?	
What do I need to work on?	Did I express myself creatively?
Did I spend responsibly?	Today's highlights:
Was I generous and kind? (to me too)	

The most important things in life aren't things. (Unknown)

Date:	Mood/Happiness Scale (1-10): AM PM
Did I spend time with those I love?	Was I fully present?
I am grateful for:	
How did I enrich my spiritual life?	How did I move my body today?
Did I nourish my body and drink enough water?	
What do I need to work on?	Did I express myself creatively?
Did I spend responsibly?	Today's highlights:
Was I generous and kind? (to me too)	

Be very careful about what you think. Your thoughts run your life. (Proverbs)

| Date: | Mood/Happiness Scale (1-10): |
	AM PM
Did I spend time with those I love?	Was I fully present?
I am grateful for:	
How did I enrich my spiritual life?	How did I move my body today?
Did I nourish my body and drink enough water?	
What do I need to work on?	Did I express myself creatively?
Did I spend responsibly?	Today's highlights:
Was I generous and kind? (to me too)	

When sleeping women wake, mountains move. (Chinese Proverb)

Date:	Mood/Happiness Scale (1-10):
	AM PM
Did I spend time with those I love?	Was I fully present?
I am grateful for:	
How did I enrich my spiritual life?	How did I move my body today?
Did I nourish my body and drink enough water?	
What do I need to work on?	Did I express myself creatively?
Did I spend responsibly?	Today's highlights:
Was I generous and kind? (to me too)	

Be not afraid of growing slowly; be afraid only of standing still.
(Chinese Proverb)

Date:	Mood/Happiness Scale (1-10):
	AM PM
Did I spend time with those I love?	Was I fully present?
I am grateful for:	
How did I enrich my spiritual life?	How did I move my body today?
Did I nourish my body and drink enough water?	
What do I need to work on?	Did I express myself creatively?
Did I spend responsibly?	Today's highlights:
Was I generous and kind? (to me too)	

The best way to predict the future is to create it. (Abraham Lincoln)

| Date: | Mood/Happiness Scale (1-10): |
	AM PM
Did I spend time with those I love?	Was I fully present?

I am grateful for:

How did I enrich my spiritual life?	How did I move my body today?

Did I nourish my body and drink enough water?

What do I need to work on?	Did I express myself creatively?

Did I spend responsibly?	Today's highlights:

Was I generous and kind? (to me too)	

The most common form of despair is not being who you are.
(Soren Kierkegaard)

REVIEW OF LAST WEEK

How balanced was my time? (work/family/Me)	Did I get outside every day for fresh air?
Did I have the support I needed?	Did I ask for help when I needed it?

Did I remember my intentions from last week?

Did I spend enough time being unplugged?

I am proud that I....

Notes:

WEEKLY CHECK-IN

My Intention for Next Week:

I would like to:

Experience...

Let go of...

Feel...

Learn to...

Stop...

I want more of...	I want less of...

Date:	Mood/Happiness Scale (1-10):
	AM PM
Did I spend time with those I love?	Was I fully present?
I am grateful for:	
How did I enrich my spiritual life?	How did I move my body today?
Did I nourish my body and drink enough water?	
What do I need to work on?	Did I express myself creatively?
Did I spend responsibly?	Today's highlights:
Was I generous and kind? (to me too)	

Happiness is not a state to arrive at but a manner of traveling.
(Margaret Lee Runbeck)

Date:	Mood/Happiness Scale (1-10): AM PM
Did I spend time with those I love?	Was I fully present?

I am grateful for:

How did I enrich my spiritual life?	How did I move my body today?

Did I nourish my body and drink enough water?

What do I need to work on?	Did I express myself creatively?

Did I spend responsibly?	Today's highlights:
Was I generous and kind? (to me too)	

_____
_____
_____
_____
_____
_____
_____
_____
_____
_____
_____
_____
_____
_____
_____
_____
_____
_____
_____
_____

Some people will always throw stones in your path. It depends on what you make with them - a bridge or a wall. Remember, you are the architect of your life.
(Unknown)

Date:	Mood/Happiness Scale (1-10):
	AM PM

Did I spend time with those I love?	Was I fully present?

I am grateful for:	

How did I enrich my spiritual life?	How did I move my body today?

Did I nourish my body and drink enough water?	

What do I need to work on?	Did I express myself creatively?

Did I spend responsibly?	Today's highlights:
Was I generous and kind? (to me too)	

Whatever you can do or dream you can, begin it. Boldness has genius, power and magic in it. (Johann Wolfgang von Goethe)

Date:	Mood/Happiness Scale (1-10):
	AM PM

Did I spend time with those I love?	Was I fully present?

I am grateful for:

How did I enrich my spiritual life?	How did I move my body today?

Did I nourish my body and drink enough water?

What do I need to work on?	Did I express myself creatively?

Did I spend responsibly?	Today's highlights:
Was I generous and kind? (to me too)	

It is not only for what we do that we are held responsible,
but also for what we do not do. (Moliere)

Date:	Mood/Happiness Scale (1-10): AM PM
Did I spend time with those I love?	Was I fully present?
I am grateful for:	
How did I enrich my spiritual life?	How did I move my body today?
Did I nourish my body and drink enough water?	
What do I need to work on?	Did I express myself creatively?
Did I spend responsibly?	Today's highlights:
Was I generous and kind? (to me too)	

The soul has been given its own ears to hear things that
the mind does not understand. (Rumi)

Date:	Mood/Happiness Scale (1-10):
	AM PM

Did I spend time with those I love?	Was I fully present?

I am grateful for:	

How did I enrich my spiritual life?	How did I move my body today?

Did I nourish my body and drink enough water?	

What do I need to work on?	Did I express myself creatively?

Did I spend responsibly?	Today's highlights:
Was I generous and kind? (to me too)	

I hear and I forget. I see and I remember. I do and I understand. (Confucius)

Date:	Mood/Happiness Scale (1-10):
	AM PM
Did I spend time with those I love?	Was I fully present?
I am grateful for:	
How did I enrich my spiritual life?	How did I move my body today?
Did I nourish my body and drink enough water?	
What do I need to work on?	Did I express myself creatively?
Did I spend responsibly?	Today's highlights:
Was I generous and kind? (to me too)	

Our past, our present and whatever remains of our future, absolutely depend on what we do now. (Sylvia Earle)

REVIEW OF LAST WEEK

How balanced was my time? (work/family/Me)	Did I get outside every day for fresh air?
Did I have the support I needed?	Did I ask for help when I needed it?

Did I remember my intentions from last week?

Did I spend enough time being unplugged?

I am proud that I....

Notes:

WEEKLY CHECK-IN

My Intention for Next Week:

I would like to:

Experience...

Let go of...

Feel...

Learn to...

Stop...

I want more of...	I want less of...

Date:	Mood/Happiness Scale (1-10): AM PM
Did I spend time with those I love?	Was I fully present?

I am grateful for:

How did I enrich my spiritual life?	How did I move my body today?

Did I nourish my body and drink enough water?

What do I need to work on?	Did I express myself creatively?
Did I spend responsibly?	Today's highlights:
Was I generous and kind? (to me too)	

The only person you are destined to become is the person you decide to be.
(Ralph Waldo Emerson)

| Date: | Mood/Happiness Scale (1-10): |
| | AM   PM |

| Did I spend time with those I love? | Was I fully present? |

I am grateful for:

| How did I enrich my spiritual life? | How did I move my body today? |

Did I nourish my body and drink enough water?

| What do I need to work on? | Did I express myself creatively? |

| Did I spend responsibly? | Today's highlights: |

Was I generous and kind? (to me too)

The Universe is not outside of you. Look inside yourself;
everything that you want, you already are. (Rumi)

Date:	Mood/Happiness Scale (1-10): AM PM
Did I spend time with those I love?	Was I fully present?
I am grateful for:	
How did I enrich my spiritual life?	How did I move my body today?
Did I nourish my body and drink enough water?	
What do I need to work on?	Did I express myself creatively?
Did I spend responsibly?	Today's highlights:
Was I generous and kind? (to me too)	

Now and then it's good to pause in our pursuit of happiness
and just be happy. (Guillaume Apollinaire)

Date:	Mood/Happiness Scale (1-10):
	AM PM
Did I spend time with those I love?	Was I fully present?
I am grateful for:	
How did I enrich my spiritual life?	How did I move my body today?
Did I nourish my body and drink enough water?	
What do I need to work on?	Did I express myself creatively?
Did I spend responsibly?	Today's highlights:
Was I generous and kind? (to me too)	

*A diamond is just a piece of charcoal that handled stress
exceptionally well. (Unknown)*

| Date: | Mood/Happiness Scale (1-10): |
	AM PM
Did I spend time with those I love?	Was I fully present?
I am grateful for:	
How did I enrich my spiritual life?	How did I move my body today?
Did I nourish my body and drink enough water?	
What do I need to work on?	Did I express myself creatively?
Did I spend responsibly?	Today's highlights:
Was I generous and kind? (to me too)	

The smallest act of kindness is worth more than the grandest intention.
(Oscar Wilde)

| Date: | Mood/Happiness Scale (1-10): |
	AM PM
Did I spend time with those I love?	Was I fully present?
I am grateful for:	
How did I enrich my spiritual life?	How did I move my body today?
Did I nourish my body and drink enough water?	
What do I need to work on?	Did I express myself creatively?
Did I spend responsibly?	Today's highlights:
Was I generous and kind? (to me too)	

A head full of fears has no space for dreams. (Unknown)

Date:	Mood/Happiness Scale (1-10): AM PM
Did I spend time with those I love?	Was I fully present?
I am grateful for:	
How did I enrich my spiritual life?	How did I move my body today?
Did I nourish my body and drink enough water?	
What do I need to work on?	Did I express myself creatively?
Did I spend responsibly?	Today's highlights:
Was I generous and kind? (to me too)	

We are what we repeatedly do. Excellence, then, is not an act but a habit.
(Aristotle)

REVIEW OF LAST WEEK

How balanced was my time? (work/family/Me)	Did I get outside every day for fresh air?
Did I have the support I needed?	Did I ask for help when I needed it?

Did I remember my intentions from last week?

Did I spend enough time being unplugged?

I am proud that I....

Notes:

Made in the USA
Charleston, SC
20 February 2016